The God
That
Claims Me

J. Anne Mauck

For more information:
www.slawerks.info

Cover Photograph and design by Jennifer Anne Mauck DeBonte.

ISBN 978-0-6151-8599-6

Let the words of my mouth,
and the meditation of my heart,
be acceptable in thy sight,
O Lord, my strength, and my redeemer.

Psalm 19:14

TABLE OF CONTENTS

BLACK AND WHITE

If only life were so cut and dried
So easily divided as two different colors.
It's a worthless lament, or so it seems.

There's a choice we are given, every day.
And once we make it, it's there for life.
But only if we choose to go to Him.
If we don't, we always have another chance.

And there is nothing so amazing as this choice!
We are always invited into His house,
Even if we decline that first invitation.
And He will always be happy to see us come in.

He wants us so much that
He does not care how rude we are
But once we belong to Him,
That one is the keeper
It's forever.

Anyone who has felt that one moment
That instant where we accept Him
It's not a feeling we want to give up
One we can't give up.

And it's better than any drug
Because. . .
It's pure.
And it's better than any sin
Because. . .
It's eternal.
And it's better than any gift
Because. . .
It's from Him.

I KNOW HIM SO WELL

We walked through gardens
He and I
And we walked through the market
Always together

I promised to be true
To remember all He said
But now that I'm walking alone
It's so very hard

I do remember though
Not so much the words
But the intent
Oh, the intent

It's not so hard after a while
When others have gathered to your side
They know the words
They know the way

We sing together
We raise our strong voices
To the clouds and beyond
So the whole world will hear

But when we are alone
Sitting around His table
I lean to whisper to a friend
I know Him, oh, I know Him so well

FLOODED

Waters flow, ebb, rise, recede
All life is tied by the tide
Life sustained by water
Evil purged by waves.

In all history
Water balances
In His favor

Moved to tears
Salty water flowing down
Raging floodwaters
Far beyond our control

In all history
Water cleanses
For His will

Crystal clear water
Streaking my cheeks
Baptism water
Leads the Spirit into me

In all history
Water guides
In His way

The river of the water of life
Flowing to us from the Throne
Leading us up into life
And up into His presence.

LEGION

I have seen the darkness of demons
I have watched a young man
I have witnessed the very evil
     Jesus caused to be cast out.

There is a fall to madness of sorts
Where man no longer cares
     for any but himself.
The importance of the soul
     falls away
          betrayed by the sense of pleasure.

Not the denial of happiness.
     That is not God's desire.
This was the denial of restraint,
     of that which makes us human.

Rather, it is the utter and total surrender
     to lust, greed, sin,
Without the care for the soul
     life, family, or God.

The demon's claws are like razors
     too sharp to hurt at first
     until it is too late.

My God is my fortress, my safety
But where one crack exists
     temptation may enter.
And one temptation leads to another.

An angel may dance
     on the head of a pin,
But all the demons of the world
     can fill a thimble
          if that's how small they must be.

THE TASTE OF BREAD

It is broken
and passed to me,
Filled with promise
that I dare to hope for.
The bread of life,
He says,
broken for you,
And I fear the taste.
I want it, need it.
But, though the smell
is so inviting.
It is the promise
that bids me near.
Fresh bread,
at any time,
to feed my heart,
my starving soul.
So I am never left
again alone in my hunger.

MY MASTER'S FEET

His sandals are worn
    from walking this land
His feet are dirty
    covered with the grains of the earth.

Though I am bathed
    head to toe
He is cleaner than I
    and I feel it.

My sins and misdeeds
    choke the air around me
While I smell the sweetest flowers
    at His toes.

I would wash His feet
    but I feel unworthy
Instead, He cleans me,
    flesh and spirit.

The waters of my baptism
    run clear
And after He is finished
    they run clearer still.

I see Him, clean and whole now
    from head to foot
But His feet will seem dirty to you
    from the long walk to your heart.

IN SORROW

It is not only in sorrow
Not just in the death wound
That my God breathes

Every breath fills my spirit
Every breeze a comfort
Every moment in His presence.

I falter daily
I regret my weakness
Then is the time He is strong.

It is in my joy that
He wants me, and
In joy that He feeds me.

Yet in that sorrow
When I seek
His joy is given and received.

In sorrow and in joy
In stillness and in the storm
He is my bed, my boat,
My kerchief, and my laughter.

WHEN THE DEVIL COMES A CALLIN'

When the Devil comes a callin'
    he rings the bell and runs.
Other times, he's dressed to the nines
    quotin' Scripture with the best.

The Devil denies faith
    he wants proof
Because faith is our only defense
    against his sales pitch.

The Devil has a sweet tongue
    He could sell sunglasses to a blind man
        at night.
His words are smooth;
    they go down easy
    but they stick inside.

And worst of all, the Devil knows us.
    He could sell a song to a deaf man
        with only a promise to hear it one day.

Ask yourself this –
    who was it who gave
    the blind man sight
    the dead girl life.

When the Devil comes a callin'
    know his price
Jesus gives his gifts for free.

DOMINION

I long to be free
        away from the rush
In the quiet of night
        all the day long.

I am so tired
        of these knots that hold
Where sin binds me
        and all seems lost.

I become bound
        so very tightly
That I can barely breathe
        or escape past modes.

Those moments
        when You shadow me.
Soothe my fraying sanity
        and bandage my heart.

And yet I am more surely fettered
        in Your love and guidance
Than ever I was in sin and death,
        but rather with a golden chain.

To lead me home
        that I may follow
So that I will always find
        a place of peace.

IT'S A GOD THING

My mom likes to say
It's a God thing
When things turn out just right.

We don't need luck
Or wishes
Or magic because
       It's a God thing.

Meant to be. . . sure
       It's a God thing
Seems like fate. . . sure
       It's a God thing

When I wasn't seeking Him
He chose to call me
That's when I was ready to listen
I just didn't know it yet.
It was so simple,
       It had to be a God thing.

So simple, like His love and His will
Like these words he gives to me
To pass on
       It's a God thing
And I know you know.

So simple and yet so incredibly awesome
Words are the most inadequate tool
Yet all I have.

This God thing is the one thing
That passes through the ages
That we can share with anyone.

I'm ready to be persecuted for Him
You may speak all the false evil you desire
Against me for His sake.
Because I know
       It's a God thing.

And I am not scared anymore
When I hear of war or trouble
Because He promised that I would.
And whether or not my safety is assured
My soul is and I know it to be true because
It's a God thing.

INCARNATIONAL

Let our evangelism
    O Lord
Be real and true

Not a ploy
    O Lord
To only open a door

But also for ourselves
    O Lord
That we may embody You

So we live the good news
    O Lord
By that, presenting Your glory

Allow us to burn with Spirit
    O Lord
Our lives a candle of baptism

EMPTY

In the hours of solitude
    during the day's course
I stand before the world
    and feel desolate.
I look upon my work
    and feel no joy from it.
These hours seem a waste,
    devoid of hope and life.

As I lay alone in bed
    desperately trying to dream
I cannot sleep a wink
    for wondering about tomorrow.
And I talk to myself
    considering my worth
These hours deepen the void
    where all I see is nothing.

When I awake each morning
    the birds and sky rejoicing
I feel empty of all delight
    and begin to trudge through the day.
Where I seek and search
    for answers to my questions
I can hear them echoing
    as in a stone cavern.

By chance, a passerby inspires
    Look deeper, listen deeper
        hold steady, wait . . .

The echoes, the empty
    the tears, the questioning
        the joy. . . the answer

I am the tomb --
    not empty, but full of hope
        the answer to a promise
        too soon forgotten

He echoes here
He was here -- and He is still
The empty is His vow of fulfillment
and I think I'm ready
to look, to listen, to think
to remember and to trust.

PAYING ATTENTION

It's hard to hear the message
sometimes
through the words
When it's aimed right at us
it's instinct to dodge.

Even when it doesn't seem we fit
sometimes
the mold is reversed
And He makes things fit to us
in spite of our contortions.

It may take a long time
sometimes
even all our lives
For us to recognize the best
in ourselves, that He already sees.

FULL TRUTH

Until the End
    we sit in doubt
        consoled by faith
           full of wonder.

The newborn, the minister
The mother, the father
None can know the
    full truth of God.

Until the day
    when we are called home
        none will know wholly
           the full truth of God.

The student, the teacher
The cynic, the disciple
All are full of wonder
    at the gift of faith.

FLAW

A perfect church
>no mortal can know
Until we sit again with Christ.

Though made by His word
>the nature of man is flaw
By being cast out of Eden

It is not flaw
>that makes us weak
It is not flaw
>that condemns us.

The flaw causes us
>to be strong.
The flaw causes us
>to seek God.

To know a higher purpose
To hear a higher call
>than those set by flaw
Is a divine gift.

SOULSICK

Drowned out by sound
Smothered in heat
Laying down is too easy
All I want is to rest

Sick with sin
Sick with sorrow
And too weary to walk further

I would surrender if I could
But no one would carry on for me
And this sin is so heavy

Each time I lie
Each time I swear
I slump further

And I am so tired
Evil makes it easy
To continue that way

Each is a link in a chain
Of pain and illness
That binds my soul

And I am soulsick
Beyond reason
Beyond comprehension

And I am so tired
I beg of you, dear Lord
Let me rest my heart in You

BEYOND THE CROSS

Beyond the cross
  there is a hill
Climbing it takes a lifetime
  and it feels like a mountain.

Through hard work and preparation
  we each undertake this climb
But it is faith that guides us
  and grace that helps us to the top.

Each stone we encounter
  each lack of a handhold
We grow stronger and more sure
  but we cannot go it alone.

Others came before us
  and more will come after
By leaving our footprints
  they might not stumble.

His gift is the Word
  and the words that follow.
His gift is the Guide
  and the guides who follow.

When the climb is done
  and so is the day
We can rest in His comfort
  knowing we made it all the way.

THE PLACE I'M FROM

The place I say I'm from. . .
It's better than the backwater town
Unless you compare it to the love there.

I love going back there,
That place I call home.
And I never have to even leave
I am always there even though
I live in the big city now.

Everyone loved me there.
And I loved them.
I still do.

But here, I am loved
More loved than I ever thought I'd feel.
And it's more mystical and magical,
More unexplainable and unconditional
Than any other place on Earth,
Than any fantasy of love ever conceived.

It smells of roses and jasmine.
I am never lost and I will always have a home.
It makes me feel safe, like my mother's embrace.
It keeps me whole in the face of life's insanity.
And even when I die, I will still be home,
Only closer.

I WILL TRY

For thee, Lord
    I will try
        again
But only for thee.

Above all others, Lord
    You know my heart
You filled it Yourself
    With love and breath.

I know I have held in
    at the wrong times
And let it all go
    at the worst times.

But I'm ready, Lord
    to try again
I'll not close you out
    in my anger and disgust.

It is solely my loss
    when I do so
And I feel it soul-ly
    whether I admit it or not.

STIGMA, STIGMATA

The Wounds of Christ
His blood truly poured out for us
And yet we are ridiculed for
A simple Belief, Faith
Unending promises
Made without restriction

Our Father has done for us
What he could not ask us to do
For him, though he has
Ask Abraham and Isaac
The gift of a son, a life

I want to cry out at the beauty
The simplicity
His awesome nature
Words do not convey
Except in this:
"For God so loved the world. . ."

SHEEPDOG

A voice thundered from heaven
Echoing in the souls of men
Who will watch my flock?

Amidst sideways glances
and guiltily bowed heads
One raised head and cocked ear.

The voice that arose to acknowledge
was timid, wavering at first
but grew in strength and surety.

Faith had made him answer
This faith had made him courageous.
That faith would do much more.

To that new found voice
the flock would turn and follow
For it could only lead to the Gates.

The owner of the voice would
open doors, guide feet,
give comfort in an earthly tone for all.

And when his job is done.
when the people need him no more
The Shepherd will say "well done."

CRUCIFY HIM

I didn't want to,
>how could I watch
I shouldn't have been there.

I'd seen it before,
>and after too
The drag marks on the streets. . .

It should have been different
>I knew Him.
I loved Him.

This time I watched,
>followed through the streets
And the old feelings welled up.

There on the hill
>we all watched
Some helpless, some helpful.

And as the crowd shouted,
>so did I:
Crucify Him!

At war inside
>tears falling
Crucify Him!

Knowing why He bled
>knowing why He died
Crucify Him!

When He spoke at last
>begging for our forgiveness
The words turned.

Crucify Him!
>that I may be forgiven.
Crucify Him!

That I may live forever
>Crucify Him!

That I should be clean, loved.

Crucify Him!
      That I may stay with him.
Crucify Him!

For me.

TO RAISE

I keep looking down, dragging my feet.
And I can't look up
      out of shame, fear, hope
          I don't know.

Though I have nothing to lose, only soul to gain
It pains me to shift
      and I know it pains You too,
          that I do know.

I can't live this way anymore, it's not enough
I ache too much to stay
      and I can raise my head
          when You raised so much more.

HE WAS THERE

The day I breathed my first
  He was there.
I know that when I breathe my last
  He will be there.

Where men take up swords
  He is there
But here, in this place
  this holy place
Where is He?

But that day, I felt him
  He was there again
And He was pleased to be invited
  after being shut out for so long
And so wrongly, too.

And even though I was tired
  the joy I felt was clear on my face.
I smiled at seeing and feeling
  His glory again.

And in spite of everything
  I'm going to hold that door open
No matter what I have to do
  or where I have to go
Because where He is,
  there is where I want to be.

BIRTH

I held my breath
       I wanted to hear
The first cry the child loosed.

In that moment
       I knew salvation
For my battered heart and soul.

I knew I could change
       become someone of worth
Because of this life.

And I want to
       and I have to
And I am called to.

For the Son
       for a daughter
I have purpose.

FISHERMAN

Cast aside your net.
Open your arms wide.
Speak Truth to all.
I have called you to them.
And opened their hearts to you.

A COMMUNION

Before the table is set
Before the meal is prepared
We are invited
       to sit in peace
       to lay down our cares
       to come as family together.

Before we come to dine
Before we rest our weary feet
We must trust
       to forgive ourselves
       to open our hearts
       to realize our faults.

At the supper
Around the table
We should remember
       our invitation
       His sacrifice
       our forgiveness.

After we are fed
When we are full
We must remain
       thankful
       hopeful
       loveful.

After we leave His table
When the world falls in again
We cannot forget
       to continue His work
       to spread His word
       to go out in peace.

A FACE IN THE SMOKE

I have seen the Face of Evil
Though this is not the first time
It is the most definite
I felt mortal terror
Pure evil existing in this world
without denial

Falling to my knees, I pray
Protect me, my Lord, from this!
Shield my heart from this evil
such a thing that has only touched me,
influenced me gently before!

I shudder, not being able to
shake the feeling of being watched
I am afraid of it, and I cannot run.
I know there is nothing to be fearful of
Because You have me, I have You.

But actual, undeniable evidence of this
Eternal struggle, for our souls, our eternity
It is so large, so beyond me
The only way to pass beyond this
The only way is to ask You

And even though You will never deny me
And You will always hold me close
It towers so far above me and
I am so small. . .
Naught but a child. . .
Your child.

PERFECT DAY

Today I beheld the sunrise and the sunset.
What beauty You have given us!

The air was clear, the sun was bright.
What joy You have filled me with!

I walked through Your creation,
Felt Your peace in my soul,
Was stirred by the complex simplicity.

Each leaf has Your name written on it,
Each deer Your blessing,
Each squirrel Your humor.

It was a good day to behold You,
To listen from my heart to You.

That sunset was so golden
I thought I might die from beholding it.
I was sure that it was but the echo of Your radiance.

By watching the night sweep across the sky
I felt safe, protected, loved.
The stars blinked as your angels watched.
And I was there to behold it.

Each day should be thus,
A reminder of You.
Each love should echo so,
A step towards You.

That sunset will be there tomorrow night
For as long as You allow it.
I will thank You for each day you bless,
Endeavoring to share it.

INTENTIONS

When the road to hell
is paved in gold
Each step is marked
by the weight of our passing.

But no matter our intent
No matter what we see
It is what we do
that is weighed in our souls.

The dragon's breath scorches
The goat's hoof bruises
But the marks are not seen.
They cause us to stumble.

To falter, to desire
They make us want.
From want to intent
A mere slide in perception.

Fear, and fear mightily
For our God is
Far more intent on us
Than we ever were on Him.

A MATTER OF LIVING

When the weight of each day
Bears down and drags down
So that all we may do at dawn
Is bow our heads in oppression
Let that act be of surrender.

The tears of stress and sorrow
Welling in my eye each night
So that I fear I cannot go on
So that I do not want to go on
I choke back a sob during prayer.

Every moment seems a grab
For strength, for tact, for air
And that life is all taking
From someone else, from myself
But He did nothing but give.

So how can I get through another day
This matter of living is far too hard
The sounds of the world going by
The rushing sound hurts my ears
And I'm afraid to dive back in.

But there is a suggestion there
That perhaps my life is not for living
The way I've been living it.
But rather for giving
In thanks for its being given.

NOT MINE

I listen, but I do not hear.
I falter and place blame.
I cheat to find the quickest way.
I desire only the easy.

But You, o Lord! You hear my soul. . .

I cry, but only for myself.
I beg without needing.
I take when I want.
I look only at beauty.

But You, o Lord! You cry my name. . .

I turn away apurpose.
I close my eyes to hide.
I sing a dark song to deafen.
I act a black way to deny.

But You, o Lord! You wait for me. . .

I will hear You.
I will answer You.
I promise to lean on You.
I raise my hands in supplication.

But You, o Lord! Your will be done. . .

FALLING INTO FAITH

When I thought I knew myself
    I wanted for nothing.
When I believed I was all I needed
    I felt invincible.
But when I met You
    I was swept away.
Off my feet, onto my knees,
    till I lay on the floor
The breath pressed from me
    overwhelmed by my triviality.
And still You wanted me
    no matter my past arrogance
Or bold doubts, or mile wide transgressions.
    In that moment, I fell.
I fell so hard and so fast,
    one second ticked by in that breath
Before I was Yours.
    and Yours I shall stay.

CRY OUT

Alone in my sorrow,
    I cry out.
But my cry is no test of faith,
    neither mine nor Yours.

ALREADY THERE

The challenge issued
   trumpets sounded
      a King crowned
         the Kingdom proclaimed
To you, I would say
   though you cannot see it
      and you cannot touch it
         the time has long come
Live your life as if
   Worship Christ as if
      Praise the Lord as if
         we were already there.

HAPPY SUNDAY

Rejoice, rejoice
Greet all with Peace
For He is Risen
Risen indeed!
All sins forgiven
Reconciled in love
For not only a day of rest
But a day of love's labor
Happy sunrise
Happy week's end
Happy Sunday!

BREAKING

Awash in sorrows, lost in tears
None hear the reconciliation or joy.

Fearing the worst
But afraid to hope
Bending for others
Until the spirit is broken.

Overflowing with misery, adrift and alone
The darkness of the world blocks out the Son.

Captured by terror
Shivering while hiding
Alone and lonely
For naught.

There is remorse, but often too late
Most are too ready to throw the first stone.

Guide me by love.
Light my way by hope.
Walk my feet in ways of peace.
Advise me towards grace.

By the abundance of Your wisdom, I try to follow
But please forgive my faltering along the way.

MISSING YOU

When you're gone
I know I'll miss you.
But when you're really gone
I know where I'll see you

If His love can stretch between
Heaven and Earth
And I am to be like Him
Then my love can too

You were my stability
And you still are
But only now do I realize
How close this love is to that love

I'm not as lost as I could be
Without you
Because you're still here
Like He is

In my spirit
In my breath
In my life
And in my heart

PRIVATELY

Do not stand and shout;
    quiet your voice.
There is no need
    to scream your amens.
And a hand held open
    in quiet petition,
It is enough
    for the thoughts present.
Do not boast;
    for prayer does not flaunt.
There is no voice
    that God does not hear,
And silent meditation
    is the loudest supplication.
It is enough
    that you believe alone.
Do not wail or moan;
    lament in reticence.
There is no panic
    that must be borne alone.
And the heart held open
    is a welcome sight to Him.
It is enough
    not to exhort in pride.

BLIND

When we cannot see the light,
It is hard to believe.
When our hearts are blind,
It is as our eyes.
And confession is our weakness
Seems shameful
And our denial of Christ too
Seems shameful
Thus we breed sorrow in ourselves
But remember
Jesus healed the blind
And faith pure restores.

LOVE IN 3S

When He asked of me
    Do you love Me?
I was at a loss for words
    the first time

Who am I to love
    to matter so much
Before thought, the answer
    sprung to my lips

Yes Lord, You know I do!

Again, He asked of me
    Do you love Me?
Tears fell from my eyes
    and my heart

Who am I to wonder
    to be so worthy
After thought and still crying
    I said my answer

Yes Lord, You know I do!

When He asked the third time
    Do you love Me?
The simplicity struck me
    and I had no question

Who was I to turn away
    to deny Him before
And I had only these words
    for my answer

Yes Lord, You know me
    and You know that I do!

TEARS OF BLOOD

Though I came late to Him
I remember better because of it.
And I have seen
     though not through a child's eyes
But the truth is still the same.

He cried for me
     tears of blood
And I was able to see
     and to know
          and to remember.

I sat in the hard wooden pew
Late on Maundy-Thursday
The stone was rolled into place
     We felt the rumble
The light was doused
     Not even a candle to light the way

Surrounded by darkness
A chill settled over in silence
And I understood
     what the sacrifice was
And its importance to the world
But most of all, I saw
     tears rolling down His face.

Not with my physical eyes
     did I see
But with my spirit
     so that I would understand.

So here I sit
     my own tears rolling down my face
In awe of what was born for me
     before I even existed.

A LAYING OF HANDS

Today is the day.
My life begins again.

As the day of my baptism washed the old away
And began my life anew
So it does today when I become the anointed of God.

I have chosen as I was called,
To spread His Word, and His Love,
To care for His children, to move as His hand.

And so it begins in that way.
The hands of those already anointed
Placed on me.
I hardly know what to expect,
Though I sense excitement and reverence.

There is power here,
Divine and supreme.
Better than seeing the face God,
I have felt his touch.

It has poured through the hearts and hands
Of all those who came before me
And will pass through those who will come later.

I am moved to the core
My soul reels in wonder
This feeling will stay with me forever
And better yet
I will pass this on
And it will be new each time
As strong as this
And eternal, too.

TRIBULATION

Trying days are always upon us.
With wars
and rumors of wars.
And yet I fear no more
For you promised this would come.

But it is the little things
Or so they might seem
Of personal trials
set upon us so randomly
To tempt us away from You.

I hold my breath
And cry while praying
Instead of turning
in anger away,
cursing your name.

But all I want
And all I need
is Your sweet comfort
while we suffer
until Your Kingdom.

LEARN THY WAYS

Walk not the road
　　　with an angry man
　　　　　　lest you learn his ways
　　　but listen with compassion
And walk with a light step
　　　down a road of peace.
　　　　　　Do not envy his path
　　　for the way is coarse and harsh.
But rather be of the Father,
　　　temper your will and desires
　　　　　　so to stand at Jesus' side
　　　rather than beside that fool.
Though you both be judged on similar scales.

NONE

On no grounds
And in no court
But one
Will I be charged
Or tried
For my only trespass
Against you
Was to stand
For Him

AT THE TABLE

When the bread is broken
    and the wine is served
We eat and drink as the body of Christ.

It is as a family that we
    share this symbolic food
Though each of us must come to it
    alone.

I have felt alone at this table
    hesitant to accept my share
Knowing I have not done
    all that God has asked.

Yet He offers it still
    in spite of my recalcitrance
Or in part because of it
    knowing my acceptance this time
        was wholly my choice.

As I was nourished
    at the Last Supper
So I am nourished now
    but only for coming to the table.

UNKNOWN PSALMIST

My words may not be engraved in stone,
Or gilded with gold,
Or sung with loving hearts.

My words may never be said aloud,
Or consciously thought,
Or memorized by gracious souls.

My words may forever be quiet,
Held close to the heart,
Said only for prayer, alone.

My words are in the heart,
Of the heart,
For the heart.

My words are the words said in silence,
Understood only by God,
Intended only for Him.

My words come from within,
Treasured for their purity,
Subjects of prayer.

My words are your words,
When we pray,
Or sing worship to our Lord.

My words are universal,
Not uncommon,
Not bound by language.

My words call out in tones of love,
In songs of praise,
In moments of absolute sorrow.

My words are the hope of all,
Never spoken,
But reach Him even so.

THE CULT OF LIFE

Before death
    there must be life.
Before killing
    there must be birth.
Before salvation. . .

In silence and prayer
    I beg of You
Hold open the gates
    wait for me!

Hold the ill mother's hand
    give hope to her son
I raise my prayers for them
    because You stand before death.

Your life taken
    that I may breathe.
Your life given
    that we may live.

Before my death
    there was Your life.
Before your murder,
    there was Your life.
And before our salvation
    there was Your life.

RALLY

All around the banner
Voices drowning each other out.
Awaiting the battle cry
Before surging out into the world.

But no. . .
  not like this. . .

Huddled around a broken cross
Sobs and tears washing all else away
Fearing the possibility of a false hope
Wanting to share the good news.

But no. . .
  not like this. . .

Standing proudly together
Hands and faces raised to the Heavens
Living the Word while reaching out
And rejoicing with our rallying shout.

For if God is with us. . .
who can be against us. . .

WHAT HAPPENED WAS...

Where were you?

[I took her away.]

::I went with Him
::Pulled away from you
::He changed me

I looked for you.

[Have strength, I am here.]

::I never missed you
::I fear nothing
::I changed

Why can't you tell me the truth?

[She confesses unnecessarily.]

::I don't need you
::But why would I lie

::The look on your face
::Makes me think I killed someone

You owe me more than this.

[I provided sight and truth--]

::For all that I gave you
::He asks for nothing
::The world looks different now

[A new life with faith--]

::I have a new life now
::Secure in knowledge

::With the truth at my side
::And I can gaze at the stars without fear

[Without fear.]

Where can you go? Especially without me?

::I can tell you
::What really happened was. . . a miracle
::And we are not alone

I don't believe in miracles.

[Yes, I am always with you.]

PETER WEPT

For want of strength
For want of heart
For want of spirit
      Peter wept.
For truth already spoken
For prophecy come to pass
For lies from his own tongue
      Peter wept.
And so a Man was beaten
His blood spilt on roads
With His last breath a prayer
      And Peter wept still.

HOLD TIGHT TO YOUR FAITH

Hold tight to your faith
    when the shaking comes.
But do not hold blindly
    rather with thought, heart, and hope.

The stronger your shield of faith
    the more it is tested.
Never back down
    from the battle for your soul.

Our faith is most tested
    when there is an out.
The first denial is human.
The second is folly.
The third betrayal.

Do not fear the moment
    to voice your soul
Take up your banner
    sing with a full chest
Jesus is Christ!

A MAN ALONE

When he walks through this world
   seeing sorrow and pain
He is not alone
   for You are with him.

When she crawls along
   terror gripping her ankles
She is not alone
   for You are with her.

When I rise each morning
   filled with dread for the day
I am not alone
   for You are with me.

But when we are overwhelmed
   with the power of the world against us
We are not alone
   for You are with us.

When we doubt your presence,
   crushed by fear and horrors
One Man alone felt this for us
   and You were with Him, too.

RAPTURE

Take me now
Or take me later
Just take me home.
I would suffer
Hell on Earth
To go home to Heaven.

Lay your greatest test
Before my feet, Satan
I gladly take the challenge
More than happy to die a martyr
Like He did for me
At any time.

And I am willing to wait
I desire not to know when
Just that it will
That alone is comfort enough
It gives me strength enough
To stand against the storm.

Just let me keep walking
Until my time is come
Let me face Your day
Standing on Your grace
For which I cannot
Thank You enough.

ASHES

I am ash.
A speck of nothing
Lifted and tossed by a breath.
And to ash I will return.

I am ash.
Given life by my Lord.
Received of holy breath.
And to ash I will return.

You are ash.
Known from creation.
Loved from first breath.
And to ash you will return

You are ash.
Carried on the winds of time.
Moved by God's own breath.
And to ash you will return.

We are ash.
Lifeless and soulless.
Save for Jesus' last breath.
And to ash we will return.

SWORD OF WORD

I would defend thee to my last dying breath.
I shall proclaim thee from every vantage.
Grant me the strength never to deny thee.

Pen to paper
Word to heart
Prayer to God
On my knees

I will not raise a hand in anger.
I will raise my voice in song.
Speaking of peace,
Knowing vengeance is thine alone.

This gift of voice
This power of words
This undeniable strength
You bolster me always

You call me to speak out
You ask me to voice my faith
In times when faith is weak

I gave voice to my faith that day.
We were asked, do we believe?
Of all of us, only I and one other
Had the strength to say Yes!

I have heard You call.
I have not forgotten.
And in spite of everything,
Near and far,
I would defend thee to my last dying breath.

ON THE DAY

On the day God created Man,
      He also created love.
Though not so noted
      His love began and so goes on.

On the day Man betrayed,
      He chose love
Though not so obvious
      His love gave continued life.

On the days Man displeased,
      He still chose love
Though not always clear
      His love endured.

On the day Man killed
      He accepted out of love
Though he did not have to
      His love saved us.

On the day God ends it all
      He will do so out of love
Though most will not welcome it
      His love will carry us through.

On each day God gives us
      He holds out His love to us
Though many have yet to hear Him
      His love waits for you.

MAN'S GREAT SHAME

When He sent down His will,
He did not say
Love thy neighbor because...
He instructed us to
Love thy neighbor.

There is no restraint to love;
As justice is blind,
Love is even more so

I feel great sorrow, even shame
When I hear people
Make distinctions
When they are moved by
Things of the flesh
And not of the spirit

It is always the flesh
That has led humanity
To disgrace
Never faith, never the heart

A lack of faith, of trust
Is ever the fault of man
Eve felt such a burden
And could not resist temptation

But temptation
And public bulldozing
Are no excuse for
Faithlessness

And every moment we turn our backs
We do the same to God
In our endeavor to be like Him
Who walked on water
We miss the little things
That aren't so little after all.

THE LIVING AND THE DEAD

Of the living and the dead
    no matter
Just let me be of Christ
    for he judges all.

Of the living
we may sin
we may beg forgiveness

Of the dead
we have sinned
but we have come home

Of the Christ
He is a shelter
sins and all

Of the living
we sent the everliving
to His death

And of the dead
He returned
that we may not suffer the same.

IT'S LIKE THIS

So it's like this today
Rough cut, bleeding, agony
Mistakes oozing through life after life
All the same, no one learns.

So it's like this now
Nothing ever changes
Though we've seen the worst
And the best of mankind
All wrapped up in one man.

So it's like this again
Just when I thought things had changed
The honest men lie
The sweetest girls are mothers
Where are we headed if not to hell?

So it's going to be like this
The richest men will never gain
So long as greed drives the heart
But, the most lost of all of us
Will find her way.
God, bless that child.

So, it's going to be like this?
I can't change the world alone
No prayer seems loud or long enough
I don't feel that I'm being heard
Are all my prayers and hopes enough?
And are they really only heard by You?

So, I'm not going to let it be like this.
Not today, not now, not again.
I will keep on praying, yelling, screaming.
I will be heard and I will change the world
Or at least a little part of it.

So, this is it.
I have the tallest tree to be seen from.
I have the strongest arms to lean against.
I have all I need from You,
The want, the might, and the words.

IS IT ENOUGH

Is it enough
        for me to be willing
Or must I forgive
        without being asked.

Is it enough
        for me to try
Or must I go out
        to succeed or fail.

Is it enough
        to hold out my hand to You
Or must I grip You tightly
        for fear of falling.

Is it enough
        to follow in Your footsteps
Or must I also
        be unafraid.

These things I cannot do
        but for Your grace
But as I reach out
        I wonder still

Is it enough to love
        enough to suffer
                to refrain

Is it enough to believe
        enough to obey
                to forgive

I have Your peace within
        but I have my own fear
Is it enough
        for me to let go?

BE OPENED!

Be opened! He commanded.
Suddenly sight was there
    sound was there
        and the Word was there.

He commands me now
    Be opened!
And His vision is there
    and His words are there
        and His love is here.

I can do no less
    than voice what is here
        in my heart, spirit, soul.

I allow myself to be open
Suddenly I see
    I hear
        and I feel.

And the words pour out
    like water from a vessel
to filter down into hearts
    to find resonance in the soul
to do no less than to inspire others
    to see, to hear, to be opened!

REDISCOVERY

For many days and weeks
    I denied myself the sunrise
I lacked the strength and the will
    to rise and face the day.

I have not missed everything
    though it seems I've tried
I am constantly in awe
    of all You have wrought.

The rain and the flood
    my breath catches as I stare
The lightning and the thunder
    I simply behold.

The laughter of two sisters
    I smile and laugh too.
The play of a housecat
    I join in with delight.

I allowed hate and anger
    to blind me too long.
I denied myself your comfort
    to hold onto evil.

I stopped listening and
    I stopped speaking and
        I fell.

And now I hurt.
I was jolted awake
    into a different world.

Like the urban fox
    not the world I should know
But one filled with concrete and cars
    and with swords and bombs
No woods for my home
    save the ones left by grace.

SIGNS

I prayed for a sign
  dear Lord
    and you answered

I questioned a mortal call to my spirit
I asked for your guidance
  to fill me with
    your spiritual burning
      if this should be

And you gave me your answer
though my heart did not burn
    and my soul did not tug me
      I knew . . .

The stillness and silence
The lack of doubt
And freedom from guilt
I asked for a sign and
  in Your giving
    you gave me none
      and I found my peace there.

NAUGHT BUT A FRAUD

Every word, every movement
They sound and look right
but feel so wrong.

They don't quite fit me
Though I want them to.
So why have You given them to me?

There are nights when I want to scream out
Why me, Lord?!?
But, I don't.

I let the words flow through me
    my heart
from You
while tears flow down my face from the blinding purity.

The ache though, it's not quite pain.
It's from trying to hold in a gift
    I know I must share.
but still, I wonder
    Why me, through such a seeming fraud?

THE GRACE OF FAITH

For want of Your grace
I burn in the torment of hate.
I punish myself for
   deeds not my own.
I carry the burdens of another's soul.

I have tried
   and I have failed.
I fear for his heart, his soul,
   his wife, and his son.
But I have tried.

The thorns of mortal life
   have grown up between us.
I doubt he ever heard You,
   much less my own voice.

And I feel abandoned
   by the animal
   that was once a man,
   once a friend.

But I also know You.
I have faith that there is a lesson here.
Even if that lesson is only faith.

THE ACHE

I ache
I anger
I rage
and I cannot hear You.

I am betrayed
I am hurt
I am lonely
and I need Your comfort.

I am fragile
I am afraid
I am a child
and I cannot feel You.

I cry
I mourn
I die
and I hold back from You.

My fears are irrational
My anger is unreasonable
My hurt goes beyond my heart,
      it tears at my soul.

And I sin
      without remorse.
And I hate
      without letting go.
And it kills me
      every day.

I hide it well
I hide from it too
But how do I let go?
How can I move on?

Forgiveness is easy to say
      but hard to live.
Anger is a temporary comfort
      but has a lasting price.

UMBRELLA

There is a comfort in the lightning
     and in the thunder,
in the knowing the storm has finally arrived.
A storm can't last forever.

Pain is like the storm
     it comes in waves like the wind
     it can be hidden from, in fear
     it echoes like the thunderclap
     but in the end, it tapers off and ends.

You are my umbrella, Lord.
     You keep me dry in pouring rain.
Sometimes you seem turned inside out
     by the strength of circumstance
But in the end,
     I would never leave home
          without you.

REASON BEING

I once heard a man say
That faith is easier than reason.
Even so, there is reason for every faith,
And a faith behind every reason.

SCRIPTURE REFERENCES

Particular Scripture references that inspired.

BE OPENED

-Mark 7:34

GRACE OF FAITH, THE

-Mark 4:18-19

IN SORROW

-II Corinthians 12:9

IT'S A GOD THING

-Matthew 5:11; Mark 13:7

LEARN THY WAYS

-Proverbs 22-23

LEGION

-Mark 5:9

LOVE IN 3S

-John 21:1-19

NONE

-Mark 14:55

PETER WEPT

-Mark 14:72

RALLY

-Romans 8:31

STIGMA, STIGMATA

-John 3:16

SPECIAL THANKS

Carol Mauck, my mother
> Without your encouragement, I never would have even started down this path.

Paul DeBonte, my husband
> For your constant assistance and faith; God blessed me when we met.

The Reverend Jack Wineman
> Without your guidance, my spiritual journey would have foundered early on.

Mary Griffin
> For her Christian living, and my first exposure to a holy church.

Phyllis Kesler
> For your love, hugs, and constant support.

About the Author

Jenny has been writing for most of her life but began this poetry project in early 2001. She will be the first to tell you that the words you have read in this book came to her 99% as is, as a gift rather than a talent.

She was baptized into God's family through the Presbyterian Church at age 12 and became a member of Bethany Presbyterian Church in Lafayette, Indiana at the same time. In 2007, she was married in the same church to her husband Paul.

www.ingramcontent.com/pod-product-compliance
Lightning Source LLC
Chambersburg PA
CBHW032028040426
42448CB00006B/758